fabric Craft

15 CREATIVE PROJECTS AND HOME ACCENTS YOU CAN MAKE

fabric Crafts

◆

15 CREATIVE PROJECTS AND

HOME ACCENTS YOU CAN MAKE

◆

ZELDA GRANT

NORTH LIGHT BOOKS
CINCINNATI, OHIO

www.artistsnetwork.com

acknowledgements

Thanks to each of you that have touched my life: Ken and Angel Rogers, Joy Rogers, Marian Edwards, Willie Mae Williams, Marva Grate, Vera Russell, Martha Ann Tyson, Claudette Dowling, Donna Edwards Towns, Robin Edwards, Amoyewa and JuJu, Lynn Farris, Charlotte Jordan, Deborah Shedrick, Octavia Reynolds, Ruth Weinkle, Ann Davis, Kimble Griffin, Mona Powell, Shirley Robinson, Mervin Grant, Angelo and Vivian Fraser, Loretta Green Johnson, Felecia and Huey Prince, Katie Green Norman, Mike Pritchett, Patrice Coleman, Fern Harmond, Gmerice Lamb, Rodney Smothers, M. Lynn Moore, Jeanene Williams, Gail Grate Alexander, Lucy Amey, Rel King, Cynthia "Zindi" Tate and my pastor, Eddie L. Long. I thank you with all my heart.

I also want to make a few special acknowledgments. First, to my mother, Zelma Fraser Carr, your kindness, insightfulness, unselfishness and patience have taught me life lessons as pure as gold. To my sister, Octavia Rogers Ivory, thank you for being a dear friend, my biggest fan, and for sharing your unconditional love. To my sons, Kevin and Ian, you guys have been two of the best sons a mother could want. I am so blessed to have you both in my life. And to my brother, Kenneth Dwayne Rogers, your sacrifices for me will never be forgotten. I appreciate the kind and caring man that you are.

I am most grateful to the staff at F & W Publications, particularly Tricia Waddell, Greg Albert and Christine Polomsky. What a beautiful team! Thanks for your warmth, guidance and professionalism.

I love you all.

Other fine North Light Books are available from your local bookstore or art supply store or direct from the publisher.

05 03 02 01   5 4 3 2 1

Library of Congress Cataloging-in-Publication Data
Grant, Zelda
Fabric crafts : 15 creative projects and home accents you can make / by Zelda Grant
  p. cm.
ISBN 1-58180-153-X (alk. paper)
1. Textile crafts. 2. House furnishings. 3. Gifts. 4. Interior decoration. I. Title.

TT699 .G73 2001
746—dc21
2001026667

Editor: Tricia Waddell
Designer: Stephanie Strang
Production coordinator: Sara Dumford
Layout artist: Kathy Gardner
Photographers: Christine Polomsky, Al Parrish and Ernest Washington

metric conversion chart

TO CONVERT	TO	MULTIPLY BY
Inches	Centimeters	2.54
Centimeters	Inches	0.4
Feet	Centimeters	30.5
Centimeters	Feet	0.03
Yards	Meters	0.9
Meters	Yards	1.1
Sq. Inches	Sq. Centimeters	6.45
Sq. Centimeters	Sq. Inches	0.16
Sq. Feet	Sq. Meters	0.09
Sq. Meters	Sq. Feet	10.8
Sq. Yards	Sq. Meters	0.8
Sq. Meters	Sq. Yards	1.2
Pounds	Kilograms	0.45
Kilograms	Pounds	2.2
Ounces	Grams	28.4
Grams	Ounces	0.04

dedication

To my Almighty God, what an awesome opportunity you prepared me for and a wonderful blessing you have bestowed upon me. I give you all the glory, honor and praise! I also dedicate this book to my grandmother, Alethia Fraser Flowers (1910-1999) and to my father, Coach Vernon Rogers (1925-1997).

ZELDA GRANT is a self-taught fabric artist from Atlanta, Georgia. With a degree in psychology and a background in art therapy, Zelda answered her calling as an artist after many years of unfulfilling jobs. In 1989 she started her own company, Bag Lady & Company, to market her fabric creations. As her art began to evolve, she began teaching classes and soon joined the artist roster of the Georgia Council for the Arts/Young Audiences of Atlanta, Inc., providing arts education to thousands of students. She currently divides her time between her fabric arts studio, teaching workshops to people of all ages and offering her fabric creations at several major art and craft shows each year.

Photo by Ernest Washington

table of contents

INTRODUCTION **8**

GETTING STARTED **10**

no-sew projects

Folk Art Greeting Card
18

✦

Far East Fabric Journal
28

✦

Seascape Fabric Bookmark
34

✦

Zebra Stripe Shadow Box
38

✦

Cowrie Shell Holiday Basket
46

✦

African Mud Cloth Box
52

✦

Rose & Eucalyptus Sachet
56

✦

Leopard Print Frame
62

✦

Elephant Safari Lamp Shade
70

✦

Mosaic-Tiled Birdhouse
76

sewing projects

Moon & Stars Drawstring Bag
86

✦

Caribbean Sky Pillow
92

✦

Sailboat Stationery Holder
100

✦

Tropical Fish Table Linen Set
104

✦

Holiday Velvet Swag
112

IDEA GALLERY 116

RESOURCES 126

INDEX 127

introduction

✦ This book is a conversation in creativity. In the realm of being creative, I have found that the best rule is to allow yourself to enjoy endless opportunities for full self-expression. The question is not merely, "What can you do?" My question is, "What can you put your whole self into?" My need to take the creative plunge happened at age 10 when sewing doll clothes, and hair bows became my activity of choice. By the age of 12, I had sewn my first dress—zipper and darts included. Many, many years were filled with fabric fun and then somewhere after age 20, it all stopped. I allowed other activities and priorities to overshadow my creative life. But when my creative energies were allowed to surface again, they came forth full force. Since 1989, when I started my own business creating fabric art pieces, I have been on an exciting artistic journey. I hope this book will be a short tour on your own artistic path. How many times have you had the thought, "I can do that" or "I know I can do something!" but somehow you never have? If you have the smallest desire to express yourself in a new way,

share something very special with somebody, or feel a sense of accomplishment like never before, this book is for you!

The projects presented here are in two categories: no-sew projects and sewing projects that require hand-stitching or a sewing machine. All of the materials I have used throughout this book are commonly found in craft stores or in your own home. Notebooks, picture frames, baskets and even an oatmeal box can become fabulous, fun and more functional just by dressing them up with fabric.

The availability of different fabrics varies from place to place. An attempt to find the exact fabrics I have chosen for a particular project will probably prove to be very frustrating and time consuming. I am often challenged to find the same fabric in the same place after a period of time. So, I encourage you to trust your own artistic vision when choosing fabrics to create your version of the projects. I have no doubt that you will discover endless possibilities for making beautiful home accents and gifts with the wide range of fabrics available in your area. So let the creative journey begin!

Zelda Grant

getting started

Let's get ready to create! This section will tell you where to find fabrics, materials and supplies in addition to providing suggestions for organizing your work space. And you will learn how to utilize your most important creative tool: your imagination.

creating your work space

The first step in stimulating your creativity is to set aside a space in your home for creative projects. To create this space, try this simple exercise: Close your eyes and visualize your perfect creative work space. It's the place where you can do all the exploring and discovering you wish. You can work in all artistic mediums, making things as large or as small as you wish. It is airy, quiet and well lit. At the click of a button there is music. Feel the perfect mood. See the perfect space (keep your eyes closed). Watch your imagination expand from one exciting idea to the next. Now, hold onto those feelings and thoughts. Slowly open your eyes. Can you recreate that feeling in the room where you are? If not, move to another room, and another. Continue until you find "your space." It is there.

For some of you, an entire room is available that can be transformed into your "studio." If so, excellent. However, for many of you, only a corner in a room is available. Wonderful! Sacrifice that corner as the place where you can nurture your creative self. I began with a corner in my bedroom as my creative space. That corner became my retreat and where I dreamed of exactly what I do today—create for a living! What fits in your corner? A card table or a nightstand, perhaps? Drape a colorful piece of fabric or a large scarf over it. Buy a small plant, a candle, add a clock and a lamp. Hang up images from magazines that inspire you. Make the space your own.

This is how I have organized my basement studio. Photo by Ernest Washington

Now, here's a big secret about how to tap into your creativity: SIT STILL LONG ENOUGH TO DO IT! Over the years, I have witnessed firsthand hundreds of students from pre-K to senior citizens astonish themselves with their newfound creativity. It is an adventure you owe to yourself!

Organizing Tips

To set up your work space for fabric crafts, start with sturdy containers in handy sizes rather than using one huge container. Recycle small plastic containers and use them to organize all the buttons, beads and embellishments you will be collecting for your projects. Store your containers on shelves where available and use stackable containers to maximize your space.

Store fabric remnants the same way you find them in the store, neatly wrapped and tossed into baskets or small boxes.

I roll my smaller fabric pieces and rubber band them. The larger fabric pieces are stored on hangers. Try to arrange your work space so some things can stay in place while other items are moved around as needed. Organize the space to best reflect your work habits.

basic tools & materials

To create the projects in this book successfully you will need a few basic tools and general craft materials in addition to an open mind and a creative imagination. All of the basic tools and materials listed here can be found in craft and fabric stores.

Decoupage Medium

Decoupage mediums like Mod Podge are easy-to-use sealer/preservers for most materials and finishes. (Check the manufacturer's surface limitations on the label if you are unsure.) When the medium is applied to lightweight fabrics like cotton and rayon it will make them sturdy and able to hold certain shapes. A sponge applicator or paintbrush is the most efficient method for application. You can buy decoupage medium at general craft stores.

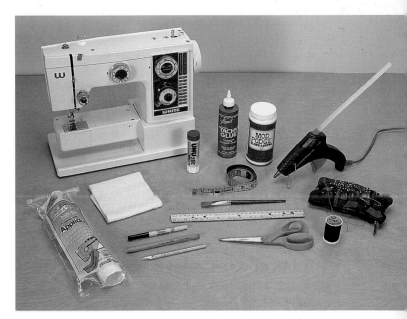

Fabric Paints

Fabric and acrylic paints can be used to add permanent color to the surface of your fabrics. To apply the paint, use paintbrushes, rubber stamps or foam stamps. You can also thin the paints with water to create different effects. Experiment with different paints and inks to get a variety of effects.

Rubber Stamps

Create your own decorative patterns on fabric with rubber stamps. Most rubber stamps are made of compressed foam rubber and come in a variety of sizes and patterns. Rubber stamps work best with acrylic paints and inks. Remember to thoroughly clean your stamps after each use. You can find stamps at craft, art supply and some stationery shops.

Fusible Web

Fusible web is a fabric bonding material that is activated by applying heat. It is typically used to stabilize a fabric before cutting, to seal a hem or attach trimming and applique. It is sold in fabric stores (and some craft stores) by the yard or prepackaged.

Glue

When buying glue for fabric crafts, make sure it is an all-purpose glue that dries clear, has flexibility and cleans up with water. Craft glue and glue sticks are my favorite glues for craft projects.

Hot Glue Guns

Hot glue guns range from mini to heavy duty. I highly recommend the heavy-duty one for the serious crafter. For fabric crafts, use glue guns designed for high-temp or multi-temp glue sticks. Hot glue seals fast and burns fingers even faster, so use with caution. You can find glue guns in craft and fabric stores in addition to some home improvement stores.

Interfacing

Interfacing is a lining material used to add stability to lighter fabrics. It is available in both sew-on or iron-on versions but it is not used to fuse two fabrics together. I have often used interfacing to change an otherwise thin or see-through fabric to a more opaque one. It is sold by the yard or prepackaged in fabric stores and some craft stores.

Hand-sewing Needles

Hand-sewing needles are available in large variety of sizes. They are used for general sewing and for those hard-to-reach areas where glue just will not fit. For example, hand-sewing is the best way to attach seed beads to a project. Try experimenting with specialty needles like the ones used for upholstery, tent making, etc. They are extremely strong and have curves and angles to accomplish almost any job. Don't forget to keep a supply of straight pins close by also.

Scissors

A well-made, sharp pair of scissors or fabric shears is a must for working with fabric. Be sure to keep your scissors sharpened regularly. Keep them clean and stored away from moisture. Scissors vary in size from thread snippers to leather cutters and a work room should have several pairs. Always keep paper cutters separate from fabric cutters. Scissors are easily ruined by multiple uses. You can find well-made scissors at fabric, craft and art supply stores.

Seam Ripper

A seam ripper is a small, pointed tool with a very sharp curved blade. It is used to remove unneeded stitches without damage to the fabric. You can buy a seam ripper in a fabric store.

Sewing Machine

While most of the fabric craft projects in this book can be completed with glue, a few require basic sewing. You can choose to sew these projects by hand or use a sewing machine to complete them quickly and easily.

Creative Tools

Once you have all your basic tools and materials in hand, remember that your most important tool is your creative mind. Make sure you have an ample supply of the following mind tools as well:

✦ **Patience**—The journey from conception to completion of an artistic project can be a long one. Without patience, it can be impossible. To prevent projects from being thrown into the closet and never finished, pace yourself. Never work on something unless your whole mind and spirit are invested in having a beautiful finished piece. Stay focused and remember that creating is a process.

✦ **Persistence**—Never give up! Practice old techniques, discover new ones and attempt to master all of them. Many times when I've been at the point of giving up I start to see a breakthrough. For me, persistence means demanding the best from yourself.

✦ **Flexibility**—Allow for interruptions in your creative flow because they will come. When you are working at home you will invariably run out of materials in the middle of a project, receive telephone calls all day, try to sneak in a few overdue chores, crave a snack, and so on. Be flexible with your schedule but serious and disciplined nonetheless. Being rigid and being creative do not easily mix. Relax and go with the flow of the creative process and the realities of daily life.

✦ **Passion**—Very little in life is accomplished without a passion to do it. Love doing what you do and put your whole self in it! Then expect to be amazed by the sense of integrity and reward you will continuously feel.

✦ **Safe Techniques**—Learn the proper use of all tools and equipment for your crafting. This will drastically cut down on accidents. Most labels on paints and glues will list precautions that should be reviewed and followed. Always take the time for safety.

✦ **"Good Eye"**—For some people this is an innate gift; for others it is learned. Either way, the goal is to constantly practice looking at things in a different way. A friend shared with me an excellent imagination exercise: Pretend you are furnishing a doll house but you do not have any real doll furniture. What things could you find in your house that could be transformed into miniatures? A baking potato tin with marbles glued to the four corners makes an excellent bathtub. A compact purse mirror becomes a vanity mirror in the bathroom or bedroom. Three small matchboxes glued together with beads for knobs are the perfect chest of drawers. And the list goes on. It just proves the limitless creativity you can unleash with your imagination. This is the one tool you absolutely cannot create without. I believe if you open your mind to one idea you've opened your mind to a million!

creativity with fabrics

Fabric is one of the easiest creative mediums to work with because there are a wealth of design elements present in every swatch. The key is training your eye to see the inherent artistic possibilities present in a bolt of fabric when shopping for materials. The creative process begins before a fabric purchase is even made.

Design

Knowing and understanding the basic principles of design will give you an edge in pulling your projects together. Once

you begin to recognize these principles, you will be able to visualize how a project is going to turn out. So much work goes into the designing of fabrics that I believe they are "art waiting to happen."

The basic elements of design are *line, shape, size, color, movement, pattern* and *value* (range of light and dark). When searching for fabrics, look at and compare how these elements are arranged in different fabrics. These basic design elements combine to create the basic principles of design composition. Some of the basic principles of design to keep in mind when choosing fabrics are:

Balance—a visually pleasing distribution of elements.

Harmony—the pleasing combination of elements that creates a sense of visual order.

Contrast—the difference of light and dark areas used for emphasis.

Repetition—a pattern occuring several times in a design.

Rhythm—the regular repetition of any of the elements of design.

Dominance—a prominently featured primary design element.

Gradation—a gradual transition from one form or element to another.

Every fabric print incorporates a unique blend of these design principles and elements. Trust your imagination and intuitive sense of design when choosing and combining fabrics. Think about what attracts you to certain fabrics. Is it the rhythm of the design? Or the mix of colors and shapes? Hold different fabrics next to each other and think about what makes those fabrics look visually "right" next to each other. Learn to trust your intuitive creative eye to find your own sense of what is beautiful and artistic.

finding great fabrics

The most popular question I am asked is, "Where do you get your fabrics?" My answer has simply become, "Anywhere and everywhere." Of course, fabric and craft stores are obvious, right? Well, have you also considered thrift stores or your own closet?

The first place to start your search for fabrics should be your local fabric stores. Look for fabrics with striking designs, great textures, loosely woven fabric weaves and reasonable prices. You'll find great fabrics in the remnant bins, which offer a wide variety of inexpensive fabrics perfect for craft projects.

Thrift stores are excellent sources for vintage fabrics, buttons and jewelry. Be creative in your choices, and don't be afraid to cut apart an inexpensive vintage dress, blouse or scarf to create unique fabric projects.

While thrift stores can offer unusual and once-in-a-lifetime finds, the same is true of your own closet. Maybe there is an item of clothing or a scarf you don't wear anymore. What about all those single buttons you save "just in case" or old or broken jewelry you keep in a drawer? Recycle it and give it new life in a fabric craft project.

When searching for fabrics, buy small amounts (⅛ to ½ yard [11cm to 46cm]) and lean toward variety. I have learned to make miracles with ¼ yard (23cm). Also, many fabrics show their greatest distinctions when taken apart. Unravel the edge of a piece of fabric or a section of trimming. The spontaneous and sometimes unrepeatable results you can obtain this way are at the heart of creating unique fabric projects.

embellishments

I consider embellishments almost anything that can be torn apart, reconfigured or used in a different way than what it was designed for. This allows for a lot of creative possibilities. Let's begin in your jewelry box. How many single earings do you have left over from a pair where you lost or broke one? Guess what? They're perfect embellishments for your projects.

When you're in a craft store, look on the aisle where miniature craft flowers are found. They can be hot-glued in clusters; add a single earring to it and you've just created a unique embellishment. From seashells and decorative stones to feathers and silk flowers, craft stores have a wealth of items that can be used as embellishments.

Have you ever gone to a hardware store to look for craft items? The plumbing department has a wonderful array of brass findings that make great embellishments. And don't forget antique buttons found at thrift stores. The list of creative possibilities for embellishments is limited only by your imagination.

The key to creating stunning fabric craft projects is learning how to look at fabrics in a new way. Successfully combining patterns, colors and textures takes a creative eye and lots of imagination. Here is a creative exercise to help you visualize fabrics in a new and exciting way. First, consider your imagination a tool. Just like a good pair of scissors, it needs to stay sharp. If you can see it, you can do it, and I'm here to help you prove it! For this exercise look at these abstract fabric designs and brainstorm objects or shapes you see disguised in the fabric patterns. Use your imagination to see the range of possibilities present in a small remnant of fabric.

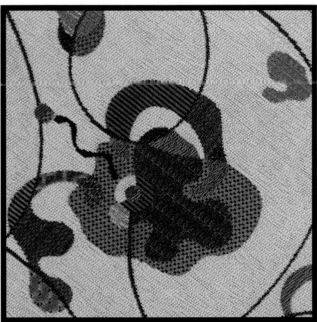

(LEFT) I see the shape of a lady's purse emerging here. What do you see?

(BELOW) It's roller derby time! With eight wheels, consider this the hottest boxcar on the track. What else could it be?

THIS FIRST SECTION CONTAINS PROJECTS THAT CAN BE COM-

no-sew

PLETED WITH A LITTLE GLUE AND A LOT OF IMAGINATION. NO

projects

HAND OR MACHINE SEWING IS REQUIRED! USE THESE PROJECTS

TO BOLDLY ACCENT YOUR HOME, ENLIVEN A ROOM AND BRING

AN ECLECTIC GLOBAL STYLE INTO YOUR LIVING SPACE.

Zelda Grant ©

Folk Art Greeting Card

Use the rich and varied textures available in fabrics to create one-of-a-kind folk art greeting cards. This is a great way to use up fabric scraps. Use your creative eye to combine a kaleidoscope of fabrics together to create different scenes. The only rule for creating these unique cards is to let the fabric inspire you!

materials list

5" X 7" (13CM X 18CM) BLANK NOTE CARD

4" X 5½" (10CM X 14CM) PIECE OF FABRIC
OR SHEET OF HANDMADE PAPER

GLUE STICK

FABRIC SCRAPS

The world of reality has its limits; the world of imagination is boundless.

Jean-Jacques Rousseau

1

Prepare the Background

Put glue on one side of a 4" x 5½" (10cm x 14cm) sheet of handmade paper or piece of fabric and position it in the center of your card. This background will provide depth to your design.

2

Visualize a Completed Picture

Spread your fabrics out around you and begin to see the visual possibilities. The house is the focal point of this card design, so that's where you begin. Decide what piece of fabric to use for the base of your house and cut out a small rectangle measuring 2" x 1½" (5cm x 4cm).

3

Build the House

Place the fabric just above the middle of the card. Notice the dark green rectangle on left. It becomes the front door!

4

Raise the Roof

Now let's pitch a roof on your new home. This tropical-patterned fabric works perfectly for my home. Find a fabric that works well for your roof and cut out a wide triangle.

5

Place the Roof

Adjust the roof to fit properly on your house by trimming if necessary.

6

Add a Warm Glow

A bright red rectangle has become a picture window. Find a bright fabric, cut it out and glue it in place opposite your front door.

7

Create the Walkway

The curve in this fabric scrap caught my eye for a walkway. Find a fabric piece that works for your walkway, cut it out and see how it looks.

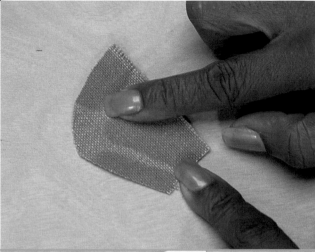

8

Pour the Walkway

Cut out the curved design and trim as needed. Angle it at the front door and let it roll through the front yard.

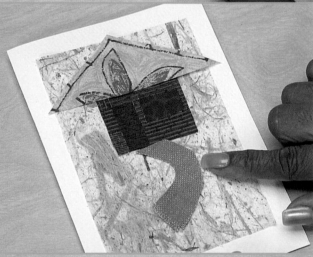

9

Use Fabric Edges

The natural, woven edge of fabric is called selvage. Selvage sometimes utilizes a different weave and color of thread, making it a great decorative element. Cut a 4" (10cm) strip of selvage to create a flower border.

10
Create a Flower Garden
Cut the selvage to fit on either side of the walkway.

11
Look for a Tree
Look through your scraps once more and decide on a trunk for a tree.

12
Plant the Tree
Cut out the tree trunk and glue it down next to the house. Make sure to maintain good proportion.

13

Add Foliage to the Tree

This piece of batik fabric has great possibilities for creating a shady treetop. What do you have that will work for your treetop?

14

Top the Tree

A 1" (3cm) diameter round piece of fabric seems to fit just right. Cut it out and glue it to the tree trunk.

COMPLETED FOLK ART CARD

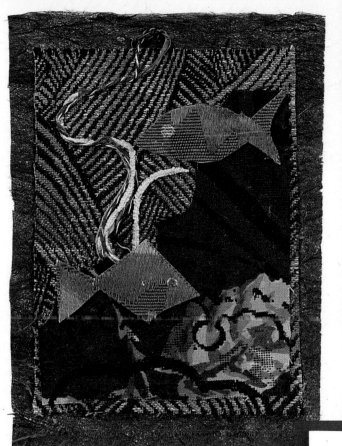

"Deep SEA"   *Zelda Grant*

"CHURCH HOUSE"   *Zelda Grant*©

FOLK ART CARDS

DEEP SEA

TOP ✦ Water, my favorite element, provided the inspiration for this card.

CHURCH HOUSE

BOTTOM ✦ This card was inspired by my childhood memories of hot summer days in the country in South Carolina.

"TURTLE DANCE"

"RAIN DANCE"

FOLK ART CARDS

TURTLE DANCE
TOP ✦ When I created this card I imagined an island with music, laughter and women dancing around turtles.

RAIN DANCE
BOTTOM ✦ This card reminds me of a soft rain, pouring through the jungle leaves, rhythmic and wonderful.

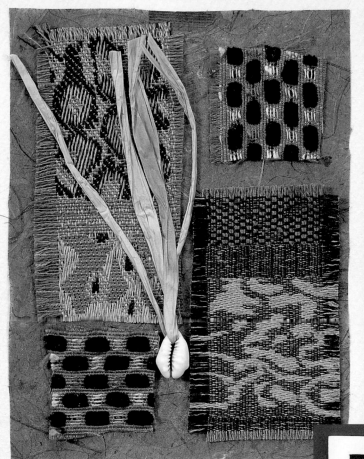

"NATURAL PATH" *Zelda Grant*

FOLK ART CARDS

NATURAL PATH

TOP ✦ This card is about following your heart and taking the path that feels right. When it feels right it usually is.

CARNIVAL

BOTTOM ✦ This card reminds me that the party is far from over.

"CARNIVAL" *Zelda Grant*

Far East Fabric Journal

Take an ordinary notebook and transform it into an exotic keepsake journal. Choose a striking fabric design or use a simple fabric and add unique embellishments. Either way, this journal is a wonderful gift for yourself and makes a thoughtful, handcrafted gift for someone special.

materials

9³⁄₄" X 7¹⁄₂ (25CM X 19CM) COMPOSITION NOTEBOOK

¹⁄₃ YARD (30CM) OF LIGHT- TO MEDIUM-WEIGHT FABRIC

¹⁄₃ YARD (30CM) OF IRON-ON INTERFACING
(FOR LIGHTWEIGHT FABRICS ONLY)

15" (38CM) RIBBON FOR BOOKMARK

TWO 8¹⁄₂" X 11" (22CM X 28CM) SHEETS OF
CARD STOCK OR HEAVYWEIGHT DECORATIVE PAPER

GLUE STICK

*Art requires work to come into being.
But unlike most of the jobs and chores that occupy
our lives, the act of creating art involves the whole person.*

Victoria Nelson

1

Prepare the Fabric and Interfacing

Cut fabric and interfacing to 17" x 11½" (43cm x 29cm). Fuse the interfacing to the wrong side of the fabric with an iron. Fold the fabric in half and press. This crease will allow you to center the fabric cover with the spine of the notebook.

2

Cut the Tabs

Measure 1" (3cm) from the top and bottom of your fabric cover. Cut two 1" (3cm) slits on each side of the binding that measures the width of the notebook spine.

3

Fold the Tabs

Rub glue on the inside of the tabs, fold over and press down.

4
Prepare the Notebook
Flatten the notebook and rub an ample amount of glue on the front and back covers.

5
Attach the Fabric
Carefully center the notebook on the fabric, matching the tabs at the top and bottom of the spine. Once you stick the notebook down, turn it over and smooth out any creases or loose areas in the fabric.

6
Set the Corners
The corners are very important in this project. For best results, fold up the corner triangle of fabric and glue it in place.

7

Fold the Remaining Edges

Rub glue along all the inside edges of the notebook and fold the fabric edges down.

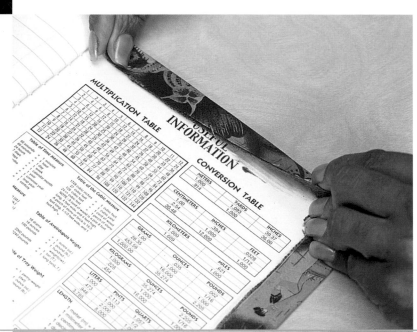

8

Attach the Ribbon

Put 1" (3cm) of glue on one end of the ribbon and attach it near the spine of the back cover. This will be your bookmark.

9

Add the Paper Liner

Create the "finished" look on this project with a paper liner. Measure the inside of the cover from the middle book seam to the outside edge. Deduct ¼" (6mm) from all sides and cut your card stock to this dimension. Apply glue generously and evenly to one side of the paper and adhere it to the inside of the notebook cover. You can leave the corners of the paper squared or you can round them off.

...ght as the secretary left, this
God did represent an achieve-
difficulties securing permis-
ch for authors and a capable

Well aft... h...
st issue of *The Lam...*
ment. Paper sh...rtage
sions, a desperate sear...
printer in a city that seemed deserted—all this had
been overcome in six weeks with the eager assistance
of this young man—and in the midst of it all
confused day of the surrender, bringing w...
and unexpected political difficulties. In s...
thing they had managed to publish th...

The Lamb of God.

He picked up the proof sheets
through his fingers one by one, bo...
would do all that, read the pro...
into pages; he laid the sheer...
title page. It bore a vigne...
had headed the title pag...
bit of kitsch; it could...
the bookcases of C...
portfolios, lay cou...
in storerooms,...
which was a...
with a we...
against...
cross...

h...
vas s...
verything...
he objected
of such small
roportioned—

ir
y, and sat down.
eries... happy and joyful,
abrup...y interrupted, and
y the other feeling, a mix-
. His gaze still rested on the
ger saw it. . . .
eard a knock at the door. He
gure from the table and set it
bookcase behind a row of large
mpletely hidden. . . .
ed out.
aw the proof sheets in the hand of
om surfaced again, an infinitely gen-
d with an infinitely gentle bitterness.
Herr Doktor,'' said the young man, ''for
he Lamb of God, they've just arrived.''
man peered at him expectantly, a pale,
w who appeared both devout and intellec-
bination he usually found appealing, but
ed him today.
you,'' he said, taking the rough proofs,
ne.''
ld tell from the odd bend of his back, an
s head, that the young man was hurt.

...nette,
...rn lamb
...wered tail,
...t bearing a
...ou to accept this
...eeded, in the face
...e Lamb of God—ah—
...d told him. ''We're ex...
...first postwar journalistic

Seascape Fabric Bookmark

Wrap a small piece of colorful fabric over a small piece of cardboard and you quickly have a beautiful handmade gift. A ribbon tassel adds that special touch. Use it along with the Far East Fabric Journal on page 28 for a one-of-a-kind writing set.

materials

⅛ TO ¼ YARD (11CM TO 23CM)
OF LIGHTWEIGHT FABRIC

CARD STOCK OR ANOTHER
HEAVYWEIGHT PAPER

12" (30CM) RIBBON OR CORD

DECOUPAGE MEDIUM

PAINTBRUSH

HOLE PUNCH

GLUE STICK

Imagination is more important than knowledge.

Albert Einstein

1

Cut the Fabric

Cut your fabric to 4" x 7½" (10cm x 19cm). Next, cut a piece of paper to 1¾" x 7" (4cm x 18cm). Rub glue onto one side of the paper.

2

Assemble the Bookmark

Position the paper ¼" (.6mm) from the left edge of the fabric. Be sure to work on the wrong side of fabric and leave equal margins at the top and bottom. Rub glue completely over the paper. Fold all the fabric margins up and press with fingers.

3

Close Up the Bookmark

Fold over the remaining fabric and smooth it down evenly.

4
Punch the Hole
Put one hole in the center of the bookmark approximately ½" (1cm) from the top edge.

5
Apply the Medium
With long brush strokes, generously and evenly coat the bookmark with decoupage medium. Allow one side to dry for 20 minutes then coat the other side.

6
Attach the Ribbon
Feed the ribbon or cord through the hole and secure with a slipknot.

Zebra Stripe Shadow Box

Create your own fabric-covered shadow box to display decorative objects and keepsakes in a fresh, new way. Easy and inexpensive to make, shadow boxes make unique home accent pieces for your walls and can bring a splash of color to any room.

◆

materials

⅓ YARD (30CM) OF SOLID COLORED FABRIC

½ YARD (46CM) OF PRINTED COVER FABRIC

4½" (11CM) OF DECORATIVE CORD

PLASTIC VEGETABLES OR OTHER DECORATIVE OBJECTS

8" X 10" (20CM X 25CM) MAT BOARD FRAME
WITH A 5" X 7" (13CM X 18CM) OPENING

8" X 10" (20CM X 25CM) MAT BOARD BACKING

32" X 40" (81CM X 101CM) SHEET OF FOAM-CORE BOARD

FRAMER'S TAPE OR DOUBLE-SIDED TAPE

GLUE STICK

X-ACTO KNIFE

HOT GLUE GUN

TAILOR'S CHALK

PERMANENT MARKER

The important thing is to create. Nothing else matters; creation is all.

Pablo Picasso

1

Create the Shadow Box Frame

Lay the mat board frame on the wrong side of the cover fabric and trace the border of the frame onto the fabric. Add 2½" (6cm) to all sides and cut the fabric cover to this measurement (10½" x 12½" [27cm x 32cm]).

2

Apply Glue to the Cover

Use the glue stick to cover the entire face of the mat frame with glue.

3

Center the Mat on the Cover Fabric

Lay the mat frame glue side down on the wrong side of the fabric. Line it up with the traced outline.

4

Cut the Foam Strips

Measure twenty 1" x 8" (3cm x 20cm) strips of foam-core board and cut out the strips with an X-acto knife. Put framer's tape or double-sided tape on one side of each foam-core board strip.

5
Stack the Strips
Remove any paper lining from the tape and make four stacks of strips with five foam-core boards in each stack. Press them together to make sure the stacks are secure.

6
Tape the Mat Frame
Put framer's tape or double-sided tape along the outside edges of the mat frame. Remove any paper liner.

7
Create the Shadow Box
Stick the foam-core board stacks onto the inside of frame. Be sure to line them up evenly with the outside edge of the mat frame. Put a strip of framer's tape or double-sided tape on the top of each stack of foam-core board.

8
Prepare the Sides of the Shadow Box
Apply glue to all sides of the foam-core board stacks.

9

Wrap the Side Walls

Lift the cover fabric up on the sides and press it against the side walls of the shadow box. Make sure the fabric is smooth and adhered securely.

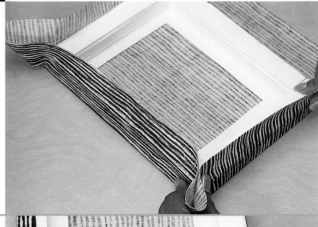

10

Trim Excess Fabric

Trim all sides of the fabric to create a ½" (1cm) fabric border that can be folded onto the back of the shadow box.

11

Fold the Fabric Corners

Pinch the corners and fold the fabric into a triangular shape to produce a neat edge.

12

Secure the Corners

Use the glue stick to apply glue to the inside of the fold. Press the corners down and trim any excess fabric.

13

Center the Opening Hole

Pierce a hole in the center of the fabric cover. To find the exact center, draw diagonal lines, crisscrossing the opening from top to bottom.

14

Cut the Opening

Cut the fabric in an "X" pattern, producing four triangles. Be sure to cut all the way to the corners.

15

Complete the Opening

Trim all the triangle pieces to ½" (1cm). Apply glue to the inside edge of the mat frame, fold the fabric up and press all the sides in place.

16

Cover the Back Board

Cut the backing fabric to 9" x 11" (23cm x 28cm). You will have a ½" (1cm) border on all sides. Use the glue stick to apply glue to completely cover one side of the board. Flip the board over, apply glue to all the edges then fold the fabric edges up and press in place.

17

Finish the Corners

Cut the corners of the fabric on an angle so the corners will lie flush with the board.

18

Attach the Hang Cord

Create a loop with your decorative cord and hot glue it to the center top of the back board.

19

Attach the Backing

Put hot glue on all four stacks of the foam-core board and secure the backing to the shadow box.

20
Add an Object to the Box
Apply a moderate amount of hot glue to the object you choose to display in the shadow box. I used a faux carrot. Carefully position it in the middle of the shadow box.

COMPLETED ZEBRA STRIPE SHADOW BOX

Cowrie Shell Holiday Basket

Embellish a plain basket to create a unique centerpiece with world market flair.
Shimmering gold fabric ornaments fill this basket adorned with cowrie shells, vines
and metallic threads for a stylish centerpiece perfect for the holidays or all year round.

materials

BASKET WITH HANDLE, 52" (132CM) ROUND, 5" (13CM) DEEP

15' (5M) OF WIRED SILK GARLAND

3½ YARDS (3M) OF GOLD LAMÉ

1 YARD (91CM) OF NETTING

1 YARD (91CM) OF SILVER METALLIC FABRIC

EIGHTEEN 3" (18CM) FOAM BALLS

20 COWRIE SHELLS

11 YARDS (10M) OF GOLD RIBBON OR CORD

11 YARDS (10M) OF SILVER RIBBON OR CORD

HOT GLUE GUN

RUBBER BANDS

STRAIGHT PINS

There are probably as many ways to get started as there are ways of chasing the blues. Use anything that works even if it seems ridiculous or not what an artist does.

Anna Held Audette

1

Weave the Garland

Weave the wired silk leaf garland in and out through the basket weave around the rim of the basket.

2

Wrap the Handle

Continue to carefully weave and wrap the garland until the basket rim is completely wrapped twice around. Wrap the excess garland around the basket handle.

3

Prepare the Fabrics

Cut the silver metallic fabric into five 3" x 27" (8cm x 69cm) strips. Cut the gold lamé into eight 3" x 27" (8cm x 69cm) strips. Gently pull two to three threads at once and fray all the edges of the strips.

4

Weave the Silver Fabric

Loosely weave the silver metallic fabric strips between the sections of garland around the basket rim.

5

Secure the Fabric Strips
Continue to add one silver fabric strip after another around the rim of the basket, overlapping each one and securing all the ends with an extra tuck.

6

Add the Lamé
Using the gold lamé, repeat steps 4 and 5, weaving the lamé strips around the rim of the basket.

7

Add the Cowrie Shells
Arrange the cowrie shells in pairs and place them evenly around the basket rim. Use your hot glue gun to secure them.

8

Add the Finishing Touches

Make any adjustments to the fabric trimmings and check to see that all the shells are securely attached.

9

Create the Ornaments

Cut eighteen 12" (30cm) lengths of gold ribbon or cord. Make a slipknot with both ends of the ribbon, stick a straight pin through the knot and push the pin into the foam ball. This will allow you to hang the ornament later if desired. Follow this step for all eighteen foam balls.

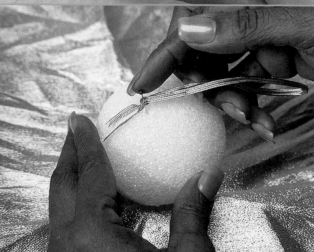

10

Cover the Ball

Cut eighteen 12" x 12" (30cm x 30cm) squares of gold lamé and nine 12" x 12" (30cm x 30cm) squares of netting. Wrap half of the balls in lamé by centering each one over the fabric, gathering the fabric tightly and securing it with a rubber band. Wrap the rest of the foam balls in lamé and netting combined and secure with a rubber band.

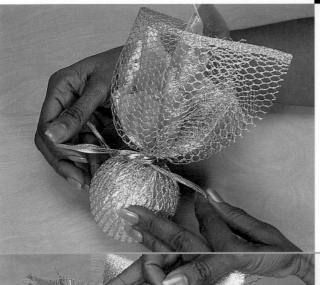

11

Attach the Ribbons

Cut eighteen 18" (46cm) lengths of gold ribbon and eighteen 18" (46cm) lengths of silver ribbon. Combine one silver and one gold piece of ribbon and tie them around the rubber-banded section. Tie the ribbons in a knot or bow.

12

Arrange the Ornaments

Gently spread the fabrics and netting apart on the ornaments. Trim the fabric if desired.

COMPLETED COWRIE SHELL HOLIDAY BASKET

African Mud Cloth Box

Transform a plain storage box into a keepsake treasure box inspired by the textile traditions of Africa.
Using multicultural fabrics is a great way to create unique home accent pieces like this box
to add a focal point to a room. A few seashell embellishments top off the box cover
to complete this natural and earth-toned conversation piece.

materials

1 YARD (91CM) OF MUD CLOTH OR OTHER
HEAVYWEIGHT FABRIC OF CHOICE FOR OUTSIDE OF BOX

1 YARD (91CM) OF MEDIUM-WEIGHT FABRIC FOR LINING

PHOTO/VIDEO BOX OR SHOE BOX WITH LID,
7³⁄₄" X 11¹⁄₂" X 4¹⁄₂" (20CM X 29CM X 11CM)

SHELLS, JEWELRY OR DRIED FLOWERS

CHALK OR DRESSMAKER PENCIL

GLUE STICK

HOT GLUE GUN

*Creativity is a spiritual action in which a person forgets about himself,
moves outside of himself in the creative act, absorbed by his task.*

Nicholas Berdyaev

What is mud cloth?

Mud cloth is the name more commonly used for *bogolan-fini*, a technique used by the Bamana people from Mali, West Africa. Mud cloth artists allow mud to ferment for several months to a year. Meanwhile handwoven cotton cloth is dyed in a solution made of pounded leaves and tree bark. Once the mud is ready, designs are applied in varying shades of mud with a spatula or bamboo stick and the background areas are dyed a contrasting shade of mud. The cloth is complete after it has been artistically painted with bleach and baked in the sun.

1

Cover the Lid

Cut the fabric to 15½" x 11½" (39cm x 29cm). Use your glue stick to generously cover the outside of the lid with glue and press onto the wrong side of the fabric. Be sure the lid is centered.

2

Glue the Sides

Apply glue to all four sides of the lid, press the fabric up on the sides and press firmly. Pinch the corners together to create a triangle.

3

Taper the Corners

Trim the corners at an angle, leaving a smooth, straight cut. For best results, gently peel the corners open, apply more glue to the box and re-seal tightly to disguise any raw edges.

4
Finish the Edges

Glue and press the final raw fabric edges on the inside of the lid.

5
Attach the Lining

Cut the fabric you chose for the box lining to 13¼" x 9½" (34cm x 24cm). Use your glue stick to generously glue the inside of the lid. Position the lining and press it in place. A fabric triangle will form in the corners as all sides are pressed up. Carefully trim the excess fabric by snipping one side of the flap and then the other. Apply additional glue as necessary.

6
Complete the Box

To cover the rest of the box, cut the outside fabric to 18" x 22" (46cm x 56cm). Repeat steps 1–4 to attach the fabric to the outside of the box. Cut your liner fabric to 16" x 20" (41cm x 51cm) and repeat step 5 to attach the fabric to the inside of the box. When the fabric forms a triangle inside the corners of the box, use chalk or a dressmaker's pencil to mark both sides of the flap where the corners meet. This will ensure a better cut and fit when the fabric is attached. To embellish the lid of the box, use anything from shells or buttons to jewelry or dried flowers. Attach your embellishment with a hot glue gun for a permanent hold.

Rose & Eucalyptus Sachet

✦

Capture a hint of fragrance and color to add to your decor. This sachet is quick and easy but has long-lasting effects. A small amount of fabric, ribbons and nature come together in this aromatic project. This is also a great recycling project. Experiment with a fashion scarf or a lace handkerchief, then add vintage buttons or jewelry for a personal touch.

✦

materials

16" X 16" (41CM X 41CM) SQUARE OF FABRIC

1 QUART (1L) OF POTPOURRI

12" X 6" (30CM X 15CM) STRIP OF TULLE

2 YARDS (183CM) OF METALLIC RIBBON

2 YARDS (183CM) OF SATIN RIBBON

2 EUCALYPTUS BRANCHES

RUBBER BAND

GLUE STICK

HOT GLUE GUN

There is no must in art because art is free.

Wassily Kandinsky

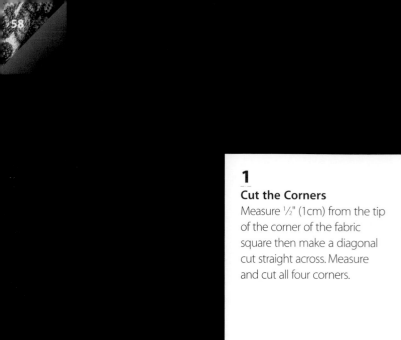

1
Cut the Corners
Measure ½" (1cm) from the tip of the corner of the fabric square then make a diagonal cut straight across. Measure and cut all four corners.

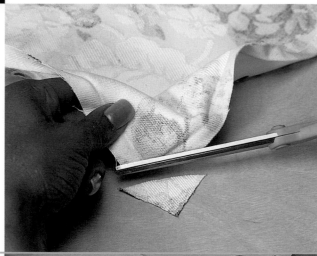

2
Prepare the Hem
Use an iron to press a ½" (1cm) fold on all sides of the square. Trim any frayed edges.

3
Glue the Hem
Open the hem temporarily and apply a generous coat of glue from your glue stick to the inside of the fabric hem.

4

Secure the Hem

Close the hem by rubbing your fingers along the edges. Press firmly. Make sure you have a nice clean edge all the way around the fabric square. Glue as necessary.

5

Add the Potpourri

Place the tulle on top of the fabric square and pour the potpourri into the center.

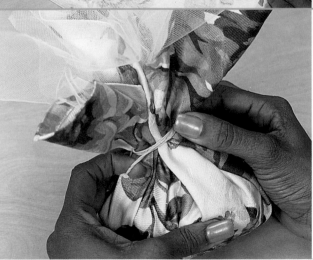

6

Secure the Sachet

Gather up all the corners and secure the sachet with a rubber band to close tightly. Adjust the fabric and tulle and trim any excess tulle if desired.

7

Add the Ribbon

Use one 36" (91cm) piece of ribbon to securely tie around the banded area.

8

Attach the Eucalyptus

Use the remaining 36" (91cm) piece of ribbon to tie the eucalyptus in place. Make two or three knots and then trim the excess ribbon or tie it into a bow.

9
Accent With Flowers
For an additional soft touch, glue dried flowers or a piece of potpourri to the center knot with your hot glue gun. Trim the eucalyptus to the desired length.

COMPLETED ROSE & EUCALYPTUS SACHET

Leopard Print Frame

Transform a plain hardwood frame into an exotic and stylish accent piece. Wrapped in a rich print fabric and embellished with feathers, beads or buttons, you can create a frame that is the perfect complement for your decor. Add your favorite photograph and it is bound to be a conversation piece.

materials

5" X 7" (13CM X 18CM) WOODEN FRAME

¼ YARD (23CM) OF FABRIC TO COVER FRAME

SWATCH OF FABRIC FOR ACCENT

1 FANCY BUTTON

3 SMALL FEATHERS

GLUE STICK

X-ACTO KNIFE

INDEX CARD

HOT GLUE GUN

I shut my eyes in order to see.

Paul Gauguin

1

Measure the Frame

Before you cut the fabric, measure the width of the frame. Add a 1" (3cm) margin on all sides. Cut your cover fabric to this measurement. Note: If your frame is deeper than ½" (1cm), add more to the margins.

2

Disassemble the Frame

Carefully remove the backing and glass from the frame and set them aside.

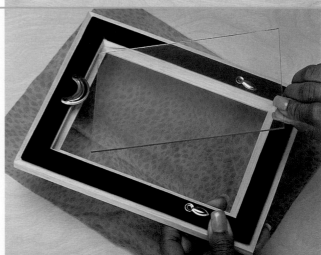

3

Prepare the Frame

Use your glue stick to apply a generous coating of glue to the front and sides of the frame.

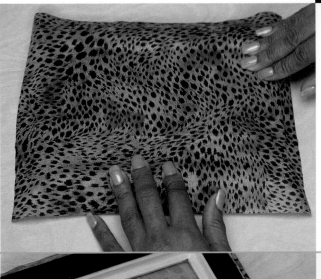

4
Attach the Fabric
Press the glued surface to the wrong side of the fabric. Smooth it evenly with your fingers. Make sure the frame is centered on the fabric cover with a minimum 1" (3cm) margin showing on all sides.

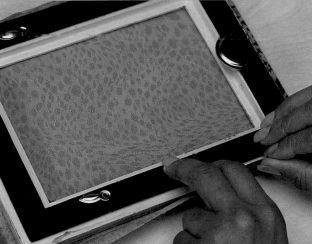

5
Secure the Fabric to the Sides
Use your glue stick to apply glue to the sides and back edge of frame. Rub some glue directly on the fabric margins as well. Wrap the fabric onto all the glued surfaces and use your fingers to smooth any creases.

6
Trim the Corners
Pinch all the fabric corners together and snip the excess fabric along the angle of the frame.

7

Trim the Back of the Frame

Trim the excess fabric from the back of the frame with a sharp X-acto knife (dull blades will drag and fray the fabric). Apply extra glue if necessary, especially on the corners.

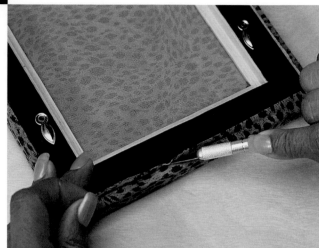

8

Center the Opening Hole

Pierce a hole in the center of the fabric cover. To find the exact center, draw diagonal lines crisscrossing the opening from top to bottom.

9

Cut the Opening

Cut the fabric in the frame opening in an "X" pattern to produce four triangles. Be sure to cut all the way to the corners. Trim each triangle to ½" (1cm).

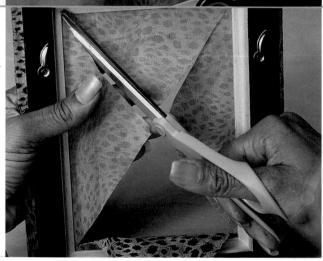

10
Seal the Edges
Use your glue stick to apply glue directly to the inside edge of the frame and press the fabric in place.

11
Create an Accent
Cut a 2" x 2¼" (5cm x 6cm) square out of the index card. Cut a 3" x 3" (8cm x 8cm) square of accent fabric. Apply glue to one side of the card and press it onto the wrong side of the fabric square. Trim the fabric edges to ½" (1cm).

12
Finish the Edges
Fold and glue all the edges. Snip the corners so they lie flat.

13
Finish the Backing
Cut a 2" x 1½" (5cm x 4cm) fabric cover for the backing. Glue it into the center.

14
Attach the Feathers and Button
Arrange the feathers as desired and hot glue them in place on the fabric accent square. Put glue onto the back of the button and position it over the ends of the feathers.

15
Attach the Accent to the Frame

Put hot glue in the center top of the frame and carefully attach the fabric accent. Hold it in place for a few seconds to keep it from sliding out of place.

COMPLETED LEOPARD PRINT FRAME

Elephant Safari Lamp Shade

Turn an ordinary lamp shade into a work of art! Add animal silhouettes, a patterned drape, decorative cord and beads to create a lamp inspired by an African safari. Place this lamp in a room where you want a home accent with an earthy but elegant style.

materials

⅓ YARD (30CM) OF CANVAS FOR
ELEPHANT SHAPES (PREFERABLY SOLID)

¾ YARD (69CM) OF LIGHTWEIGHT PATTERNED FABRIC

⅓ YARD (30CM) OF FUSIBLE WEB

1¼ YARD (114CM) OF CHENILLE ROPE

1 YARD (91CM) OF GOLD WIRED BEADS

LAMP SHADE:
13" (33CM) HIGH,
6" (15CM) TOP DIAMETER,
18" (46CM) BOTTOM DIAMETER

ELEPHANT STENCIL PATTERN (PAGE 125)

TAILOR'S CHALK

FABRIC OR CRAFT GLUE

Opportunity is missed by most people because it is dressed in overalls and looks like work.

Thomas Edison

1

Create the Elephant Patterns

Before cutting the canvas, iron fusible web to the wrong side of the canvas. This will prevent the canvas from fraying after cutting. Use your tailor's chalk and the stencil pattern on page 125 to trace the elephant shapes onto the front of the canvas. (I was able to fit three of each elephant size on the lamp shade for a total of nine elephants.) Cut out the patterns and do a preliminary layout.

2

Apply the Glue

Use your fingers or a brush to smooth the glue onto the back of the canvas shapes (put the glue over the fusible web). Allow each shape to dry for only a minute before attaching it to the lamp shade.

3

Attach the Elephants to the Lamp Shade

Place the elephants uniformly around the base of the shade. Be sure each piece touches the bottom rim of the shade and is equally spaced.

4
Draw the Lamp Skirt
In the center of the wrong side of the fabric, trace the top edge of the lamp shade with the tailor's chalk.

5
Cut the Lamp Skirt
Use a tape measure to mark a circle on the fabric that is 5½" (14cm) wider than the diameter of the top edge of the lamp shade. Cut out the larger circle and the smaller circle. Your pattern should resemble a huge donut.

6
Reinforce the Top Opening
Trace the inside opening of the skirt (donut) onto a small section of fusible web.

7
Make a Double Ring
Draw a second circle 1" (3cm) from the circle drawn on the fusible web. Cut out the ring, peel off the paper liner and iron it to the inside edge of the top opening of the lamp skirt.

8

Hem the Lamp Skirt
Fold and press a ½" (1cm) hem and secure it with a small strip of fusible web.

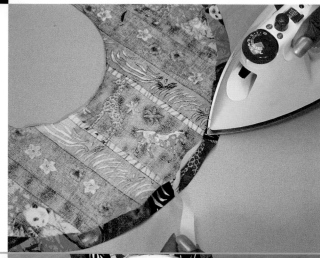

9

Drape the Lamp Skirt
Slide the lamp skirt onto the lamp shade. It should fit snugly.

10

Add the Trimmings
Cut three 15" (38cm) lengths of chenille rope and tie one piece onto each interior spindle of the lamp shade. Allow one end to hang lower than the other.

11
Fringe the Trimmings
Unravel the ends of the chenille rope to produce frayed ends.

12
Add the Wired Beads
Cut six 10" (25cm) lengths of wired beads. Twist them in spirals around each piece of the rope.

COMPLETED ELEPHANT SAFARI LAMP SHADE

Mosaic-Tiled Birdhouse

Add color and personality to an ordinary wooden birdhouse with a fanciful application of fabrics. Mix and match patterns and textures in unexpected ways to design a truly unique decorative accent. Spice up your favorite room with this one-of-a-kind project.

materials

ROUND WOODEN BIRDHOUSE, 18" (46CM) DIAMETER, 10" (25) TALL

CARDBOARD TUBE FOR PEDESTAL
(I USED A QUAKER OATS CONTAINER!),
16" (41CM) DIAMETER, 9½" (24CM) TALL

⅓ YARD (30CM) OF FABRIC FOR BIRDHOUSE BASE

⅓ YARD (30CM) OF FABRIC FOR ROOF

⅓ YARD (30CM) OF FABRIC FOR PEDESTAL

18" (46CM) OF BRAIDED OR WOVEN TRIM

NOVELTY BIRD

NOVELTY FLOWERPOTS

EIGHT ½" (1CM) MIRROR SQUARES

3–4 LONG STRANDS OF RAFFIA

24" X 36" (61CM X 92CM) SHEET OF POSTER BOARD

GLUE STICK

HOT GLUE GUN

X-ACTO KNIFE

MEASURING TAPE

The artist must yield himself to his own inspiration.

Giuseppe Verdi

1

Measure the Birdhouse

To produce an accurate fit, measure from the bottom of the roof extending 1" (3cm) under the base of the house. Bend the measuring tape to include all the flat and raised areas of the house. Make note of this measurement.

2

Measure the Diameter

Wrap the measuring tape around the widest portion of the house (this will probably be the base). Add 1" (3cm) to this measurement.

3

Cover With Glue

Use your glue stick to generously cover the house with glue using long strokes. Do not glue the roof.

4

Center the Fabric

To ease application, cut the fabric on the bias (crosswise) following your dimensions from step 1 and 2. Fold a crease to find the center, then place the crease in the center of the bird opening and perch. Mark a small dot in the center of the opening and on the tip of the perch.

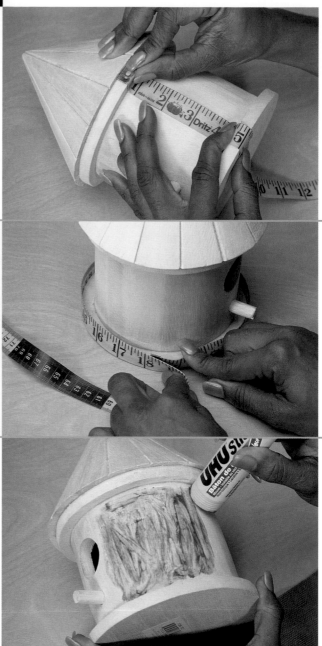

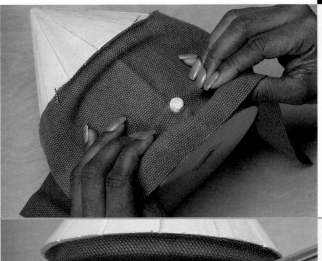

5
Apply Base Fabric

Use the X-acto knife to cut a small opening to expose the perch. Stretch the fabric over the perch for a close fit. Continue to wrap the entire house by pressing the fabric firmly in place. Add glue as necessary. As the center back seam meets, fold the top edge under 1" (3cm), add extra glue and press it down so it overlaps on top of the beginning edge.

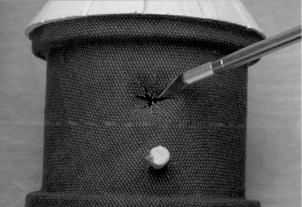

6
Uncover the Opening

Cut six slits (in the shape of a starburst) from the center dot to the outer edge of the bird opening.

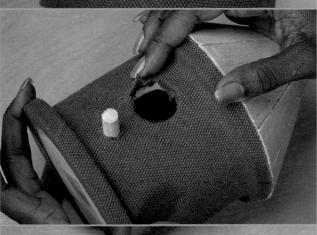

7
Cover the Bird Opening

Glue the back of each flap and press it securely to the inside edge of the opening.

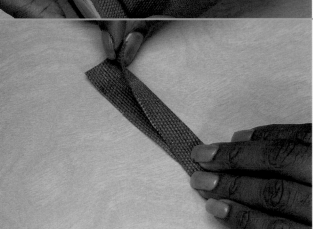

8
Make a Band

To conceal the rough edges inside the bird opening, use a tape measure to measure the circumference of the bird opening. Cut a strip of base fabric the length of that measurement and make it 1" (3cm) wide. Use the glue stick to put glue on the wrong side of the fabric. Fold the band in half lengthwise and glue the fabric together.

9
Frame the Opening
Use the glue stick to apply glue to one side of the folded strip and carefully insert it around the inner edge of the bird opening.

10
Create the Roof Tiles
Cut 45–50 1½" x 1½" (4cm x 4cm) squares out of poster board. Add glue to one side and arrange them on your roof fabric. Be sure to allow at least a ¾" (2cm) margin between each square.

11
Prepare the Roof Tiles
Cut each square from the fabric leaving a fabric margin around the poster board squares. Put glue on the back of the poster board squares and fold the fabric edges over. Trim the corners if necessary.

12

Assemble the Roof

Put a small amount of hot glue in the center of each roof tile and immediately attach it to the roof. Results are best if you start the first layer from the bottom of the roof. Slightly overlap each tile and allow the bottom layer to hang just below the edge of the roof.

13

Complete the Roof

Work your way up, layer by layer, alternating and overlapping tiles as desired. The last two or three layers will require more overlapping, bending and holding in place until the hot glue is secure.

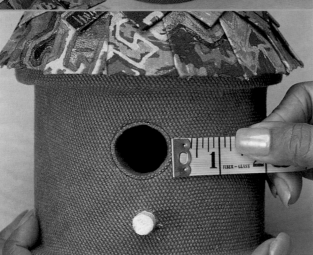

14

Measure for the Windows

Measure and mark 1" (3cm) from each side of the bird opening.

15

Create the Windows

Hot glue one mirror square on the mark, then attach three more mirror pieces around it in a square to create the birdhouse windows. Create windows on both sides of the bird opening.

16

Create the Lawn

Using your base measurement, cut a length of trim to size plus 1" (3cm) for overlapping. Begin at the back seam and hot glue the trim completely along the edge around the base of the birdhouse.

17

Add the Bird and Flowers

Put a small amount of hot glue on the perch and carefully position the bird. Hot glue the flower pots along the bordered edge.

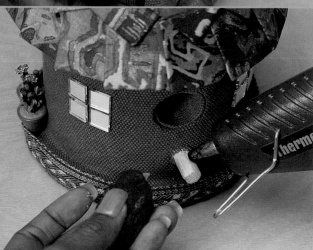

18

Cover the Pedestal

Repeat steps 1–3 for measuring and gluing the fabric to cover the base. Smooth any wrinkles and tuck the ends with extra glue.

19

Add the Raffia Trim

A raffia trimming adds a special touch. Freely tie long strands of raffia in a knot near the upper edge of the pedestal. Trim as necessary.

COMPLETED MOSAIC-TILED BIRDHOUSE

THIS SECTION CONTAINS PROJECTS THAT REQUIRE BASIC HAND

sewing

OR MACHINE STITCHING. THESE PROJECTS ONLY REQUIRE A LITTLE

EXTRA TIME TO COMPLETE, BUT WILL PROVIDE YOU WITH ENDLESS

projects

POSSIBILITIES FOR COMBINING FABRICS IN NEW WAYS. THE SEWING

ICON  AT THE BEGINNING OF EACH PROJECT INDICATES AN-

OTHER OPPORTUNITY FOR YOU TO STIR YOUR IMAGINATION AND

EXPLORE NEW METHODS OF CREATING UNIQUE HOME ACCENTS.

Moon & Stars Drawstring Bag

✦

A rugged piece of burlap becomes a delicate drawstring bag by adding colorful trim and a supple lining. Mixing rough and smooth textures makes a big impact in this project. Use the bag as a decorative accent or as a little carryall with lots of personality.

✦

materials

⅓ YARD (30CM) OF BURLAP

⅓ YARD (30CM) OF LINING

TWO 40" (102CM) PIECES OF ROPE

12" X 1½" (30CM X 4CM) PIECE OF TRIMMING

EXTRA-LARGE SAFETY PIN

SEWING MACHINE

STRAIGHT PINS

TAPE MEASURE

*Trust that still, small voice that says,
'This might work and I'll try it.'*

Diane Mariechild

1

Measure and Set the Trim
Cut the burlap and lining to 27" x 10" (68cm x 25cm). Lay the fabrics lengthwise, measure 6" (15cm) from one end, and pin the trim across, leaving 1" (3cm) on both ends. Stitch the trim in place.

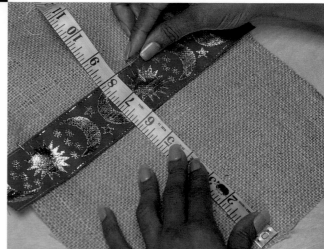

2

Attach the Burlap to the Lining
Match the right sides of the burlap and lining together and pin them in place. Stitch a ½" (1cm) seam on all sides, leaving a small opening of about 4" (10cm) along one short side. Reinforce the stitching around the opening.

3

Turn the Bag Inside Out
Carefully snip all the corners before turning the bag inside out. Pull the fabric through the opening until it is completely reversed to the right side of the fabric.

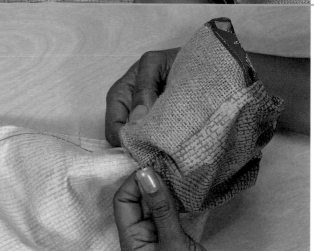

4
Press the Hems
Press all the seams flat. Flip over a 2" (5cm) hem from each end to expose the lining fabric. Pin it and press the hems in place.

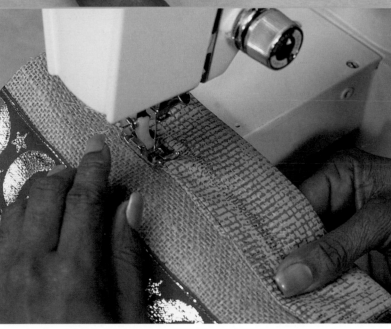

5
Stitch the Hems
Stitch the edges of the hems and reinforce both ends.

6

Create the Casing

Add a second row of stitching approximately 1" (3cm) above the first. Stitch the ends again for reinforcement. Repeat steps 5 and 6 on both hems.

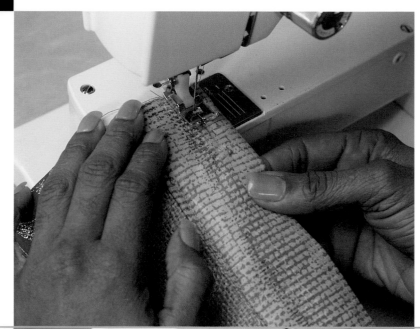

7

Close the Side Seams

Fold the bag in half and stitch a ¼" (6mm) seam down both sides of the bag. Reinforce the stitching and be sure to leave the casing area open.

8
Create the Drawstrings

Insert a safety pin into the edge of the rope on one end. Feed the rope through the casing by slowly guiding it with the safety pin. Allow both ends of the rope to extend evenly from one side of bag. Repeat this procedure using the other piece of rope beginning from the opposite side of the bag. To prevent unraveling, tie knots on all the rope ends.

COMPLETED MOON & STARS DRAWSTRING BAG

Caribbean Sky Pillow

✦

Add an artistic touch to your favorite sofa or chair with this art pillow. A half moon and a few selected strips of richly patterned fabric create this picture I entitled "Zebra Moon in a Caribbean Sky." Allow your own blend of beautiful fabrics to inspire you to create your idea of the perfect sunset.

✦

materials

½ YARD (46CM) OF FABRIC FOR FRONT PILLOW CASING

½ YARD (46CM) OF FABRIC FOR BACK PILLOW CASING

½ YARD (46CM) OF PATTERNED FABRIC FOR SKY STRIPS

⅛ YARD (11CM) OF FABRIC FOR MOON

18" X 18" (46 X 46CM) PILLOW FORM

SEWING MACHINE

STRAIGHT PINS

TAPE MEASURE

Often people attempt to live their lives backwards: they try to have more things, or more money, in order to do more of what they want so that they will be happier. The way it actually works is the reverse. You must first be who you really are, then, do what you need to do in order to have what you want.

Margaret Young

1

Create the Sky

Cut four 6" x 17" (15cm x 43cm) fabric strips for the sky. Fold and press each strip in half lengthwise.

2

Create the Back Casing

Cut two 11" x 17" (28cm x 43cm) fabric squares for the back pillow casing. Make a ½" (1cm) fold along one 17" (43cm) side of the back casing fabric, then fold again. Do this on both halves and press in place.

3

Create the Moon

Cut your moon fabric to 7" x 4" (18cm x 10cm). Draw a half circle from one side of the rectangle to the other. Cut out a half moon.

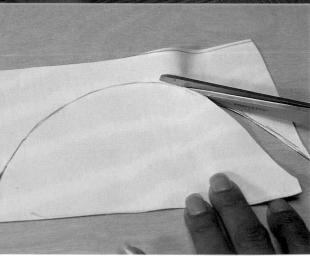

4
Attach the Moon
Cut a 17" x 17" (43cm x 43cm) square out of the front pillow casing fabric. Measure 8½" (22cm) down from the top center. Place the bottom of the moon on this imaginary line. Check the distance on each side of the moon as well. Adjust if necessary and pin in place.

5
Stitch the Moon
Carefully stitch the moon onto the front casing. Remove the pins when this is complete.

6
Add the Sky
Pin one folded strip of sky across the width of the front casing. Be sure to cover at least ½" (1cm) of the moon's bottom edge. Stitch in place.

7
Complete the Sky
Continue to add all four strips as described in step 6 until the final strip is stitched.

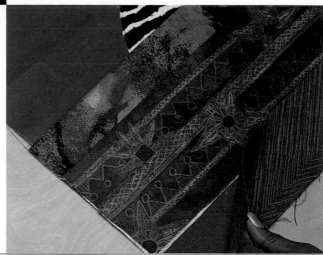

8
Stitch the Sides
Make a ½" (1cm) seam along both sides of the front casing to secure all the fabric strips and prevent shifting.

9
Stitch the Backing Hems
Make one stitch along the inside edge of the back casing where it is folded.

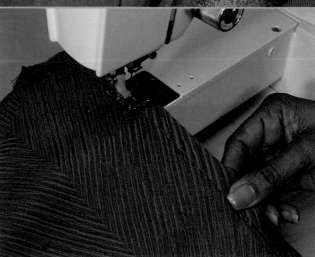

10

Attach the Front to the Back

Matching the right sides of the front and back pillow casing fabrics together, pin each half of the back casing to the front. Overlap the center sections where they meet, secure and pin in place.

11

Match the Corners

Before stitching the front to the back, be certain that all the corners are even. If not, pin and trim as necessary.

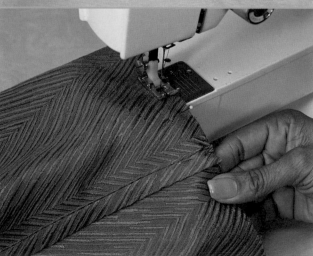

12

Stitch the Pillow

Begin at one corner of the pillow fabric and stitch all four sides until complete. Be sure to reinforce the stitching at the top and bottom where the back flaps overlap.

13

Trim the Corners

Remove the excess fabric from all the corners with a diagonal snip. Be careful to avoid trimming too close to the seam.

14

Reverse the Cover

Turn the pillow cover inside out. Push corners out until they look squared, then press.

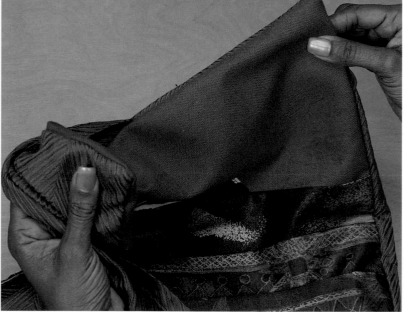

15
Insert the Pillow
Slip the pillow form into one half of the cover and then carefully into the other half. Adjust the pillow as necessary and tug the back flaps shut.

COMPLETED CARIBBEAN SKY PILLOW

Sailboat Stationery Holder

◆

Special cards and stationery will have a cozy place to stay when you create this hand-stitched holder with a nautical theme. Designed with soft neutral colors to highlight the bright sailboat, this project is a sweet reminder to take time out to write to a friend.

◆

materials

¼ YARD (23CM) OF LIGHTWEIGHT CANVAS

4" X 4" (10CM X 10CM) WHITE CANVAS SQUARE

4" X 4" (10CM X 10CM" RED CANVAS SQUARE

¼ YARD (23CM) OF IRON-ON INTERFACING
(MEDIUM TO HEAVYWEIGHT)

¼ YARD (23CM) OF LINING FABRIC

¼ YARD (23CM) OF FUSIBLE WEB

LARGE HAND-SEWING NEEDLE

QUILTING THREAD

STRAIGHT PINS

Go confidently in the direction of your dreams! Live the life you've imagined. As you simplify your life, the laws of the universe will be simpler.

Henry David Thoreau

1

Prepare the Materials for Assembly

Cut the canvas, lining and iron-on interfacing to matching dimensions of 26" x 9" (66cm x 23cm). Iron the interfacing onto the wrong side of the lining fabric.

2

Cut Out the Sailboat

Iron the fusible web onto the wrong side of both canvas squares. To create the sail, cut a triangle out of the white canvas by making a diagonal cut through the square. To create the boat, place two marks on the back of the red canvas 5" (13cm) apart. Draw a half circle connecting the marks and cut out the shape. Flatten the bottom of the boat by cutting away the rounded edge. Peel away the paper backing of the fusible web and set your sailboat aside.

3

Match the Cover to the Lining

Press a ½" (1cm) hem around all sides of the lining and cover. Adjust the hems where necessary to produce an exact fit.

4

Stitch the Cover to the Lining

Securely pin the lining to the cover on all sides. Hand-stitch only the short sides at this time from top to bottom. For best results, space the stitches as evenly as possible and remember to reinforce where you begin and end your stitching.

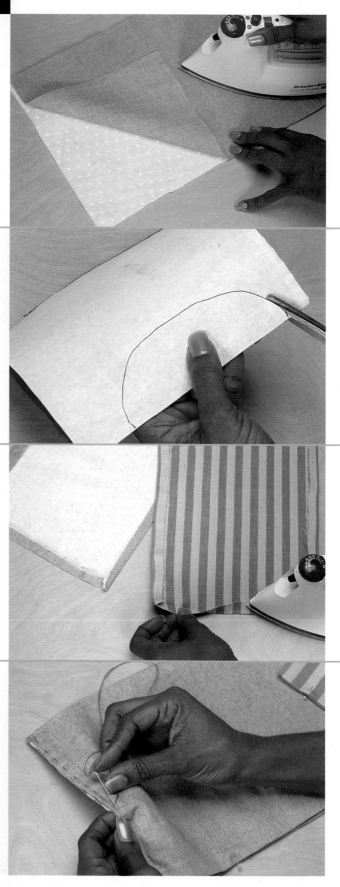

5
Create the Pocket Folds

Leave a 1" (3cm) space between the left and right sides as you fold the cover in on the left and right sides to create two pockets. Pin the folds in place and stitch along the top and bottom of the cover. Reinforce the stitching at all opening edges.

6
Attach the Sailboat

Position the sail and boat in the middle of the front flap. Iron it in place.

COMPLETED SAILBOAT STATIONERY HOLDER

Tropical Fish Table Linen Set

Set the table and the mood with these fabric-stamped placemats, napkin holders and table runner
inspired by the tropics. Created with simple techniques, this project makes a dramatic presentation.
Both fashionable and exotic, this unique table linen set will have you entertaining in style.

materials

2 YARDS (183CM) OF FABRIC FOR
FRONT OF PLACEMATS AND TABLE RUNNER

2¼ YARDS (206CM) OF LINING FABRIC FOR
BACK OF PLACEMATS AND TABLE RUNNER

2 YARDS (183CM) OF PRESS-ON INTERFACING (OPTIONAL)

¼ YARD (23CM) OF HEAVYWEIGHT CANVAS

GOLD ACRYLIC PAINT

CHUNKY RUBBER OR FOAM STAMP(S)

STAMP PAD

SEWING MACHINE

STRAIGHT PINS

TAPE MEASURE

GLUE STICK

To create presupposes love for that which one creates.

Erich Fromm

1

Prepare the Fabric and Stamps

Cut two 14" x 18" (36cm x 46cm) fabric squares out of your place-mat fabric. Use a clean, dry stamp pad and coat it completely with acrylic paint. Carefully press the rubber stamp onto the stamp pad, evenly coating it with paint.

2

Create the Placemat Design

Visualize a beautifully completed mat before you decide where to stamp the placemats. For best results, recoat the stamp after each application. Set the place-mat aside to dry for about 20 minutes.

Tip

Placing too much paint on the stamp pad readily becomes too much paint on the proj-ect. Do a test stamping with a similar piece of fabric. If the final impression does not show well, do not re-stamp; fill in any spaces with a tiny paint brush.

3

Prepare the Canvas for Napkin Rings

Cut four 5" x 7½" (13cm x 19cm) squares out of the canvas. Fold and press ½" (1cm) along the top and bottom edges of each canvas piece.

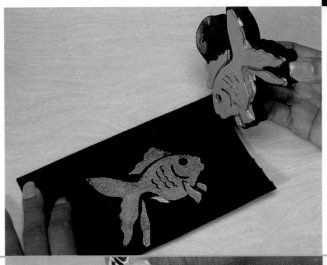

4

Stamp the Canvas
Stamp the canvas following the instructions in step 2. For best results, place the pattern in the center of the canvas. Repeat this for all four canvas squares. Set them aside to dry.

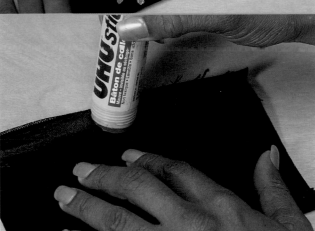

5

Secure the Hems
On the long sides of each canvas square, fold over a $\frac{1}{2}$" (1cm) hem on both sides. Use a heavy coat of glue to hold the hems in place.

6

Hand-Press the Hems
Allow the glue to become a little tacky (slightly dry) then press down firmly and smooth with your fingers.

7

Stitch the Napkin Rings

Match the top and bottom edges as you fold and stitch a ½" (1cm) seam. Be sure to reinforce the stitching at each end. Repeat this for all four napkin holders.

8

Fringe the Edges

Create a fringed edge by slowly pulling a few threads away from the stitched edged of the canvas. Create approximately ¼" (6mm) of fringe on each napkin holder.

9

Prepare the Placemat Lining

Cut two 14" x 18" (36cm x 46cm) pieces of lining fabric for the border and back of the placemats. Fold and press a 2" (5cm) hem along all sides of each lining.

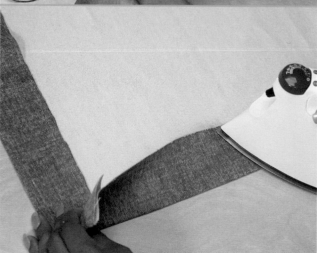

10
Finish the Lining Edge
Open the hem and fold and press another ½" (1cm) hem along the outer edge on all sides.

11
Taper the Corners
With one side opened and the other side closed, create a triangular fold on the original hem. Press in place.

12
Trim the Top Corners
Trim the excess fabric from the folds. Cut approximately ¼" (6mm) from the crease line.

13

Trim the Inside Corners

Hold the bottom tip of the newly cut edge and cut straight across just below the crease. Repeat steps 12 and 13 until all the corners are finished.

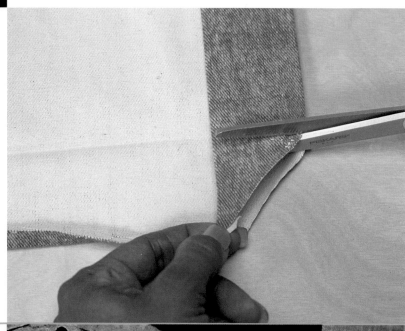

14

Attach the Mat to the Lining

If interfacing is desired for a little bit of padding, cut it to size and iron it to the wrong side of the mat. Insert the mat inside the lining, making certain the mat fits evenly within the hems. Pin all four sides, adjusting corners as necessary.

15

Complete the Placemat

Begin stitching at one corner along the inside edge of the hem and continue until all sides have been stitched. Reinforce the hems by stitching diagonally from the inside corners to the tips of each outer corner. Repeat steps 11–15 to complete the second placemat.

16

Create the Table Runner

Cut your placemat top fabric to 14" x 70" (36cm x 178cm). Cut your lining fabric to 18" x 74" (46cm x 188cm). To make the table runner, follow the same basic instructions for completing the placemats. Now you have a beautiful table set for four!

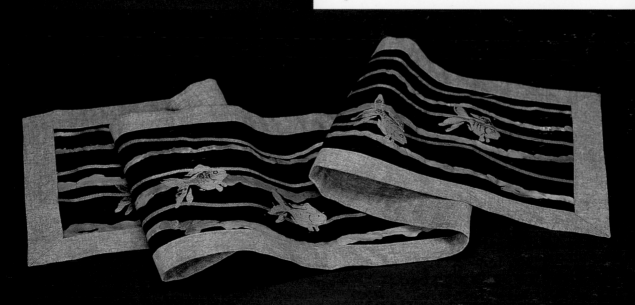

Holiday Velvet Swag

Create this sumptuous velvet swag with a touch of holiday magic. Its length suggests many wonderful uses. Use it as a table drape, a throw, a mantel swag or wherever a soft touch and rich color are needed.

materials

1½ YARDS (137CM) OF VELVETEEN
(2½ YARDS [229CM] FOR A SEAMLESS SWAG)

1½ YARDS (137CM) OF LINING FABRIC

FOUR 3"–4" (8CM–10CM) TASSELS

HOLIDAY ORNAMENT STENCILS

GOLD OR SILVER SPRAY PAINT

HAND-SEWING NEEDLE AND THREAD

RUBBER GLOVES

STRAIGHT PINS

TAPE MEASURE

You can do anything you want to do. What is rare is this actual wanting to do a specific thing: wanting it so much that you are practically blind to all other things, that nothing else will satisfy you.

Robert Henri

1

Prepare the Fabric

Measure and cut the velveteen and lining to 14½" x 90" (37cm x 229cm). Position the stencils on the fabric and spray paint two light coats to create an impression. Concentrate the paint in the area where the stencils are placed. Following the manufacturer's directions, allow ample time for the paint to dry.

2

Position the Tassels

Pin a tassel at each corner of the front of the swag. Measure to be sure all the tassels will hang evenly.

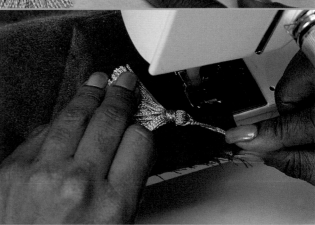

3

Attach the Tassels

Place a stay-stitch ½" (1cm) from the corner edges in an L-shape. Catch the loop of the tassel with this stitch. Repeat if needed to keep the tassel from slipping out of place.

4

Attach the Lining

Pin the lining to the velveteen with the right sides of the fabric facing each other. Put cellophane tape across the tassels to prevent them from being caught in the final seam. To discourage shifting, sew down one long side of the swag, then sew the other long side. Leave a 6" to 8" (15cm to 20cm) opening in the middle of one seam. Reinforce the stitches at each side of the opening. Lastly, stitch each side seam.

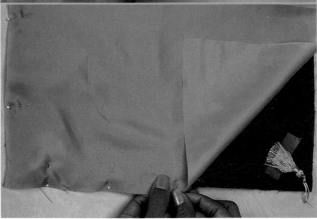

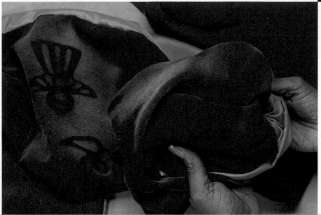

5
Reverse the Swag
Carefully turn the swag inside out through the opening. Gently remove the tape from across the tassels and tug on them lightly to release the corners.

6
Press the Seams
With a warm iron, press the seams of the opening so they are even. The entire swag may also be pressed at this time.

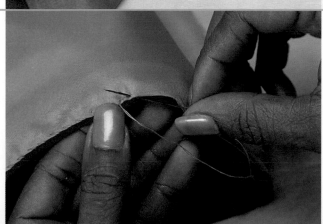

7
Close the Opening
Use the hand-sewing needle to make simple slip stitches to close the opening. Be careful not to pull the threads too tightly.

COMPLETED HOLIDAY VELVET SWAG

idea gallery

INSPIRATION CAN COME FROM ANY PLACE AT ANY TIME. NOW THAT YOU HAVE TRIED SOME OF THE STEP-BY-STEP PROJECTS, FIND YOUR OWN CREATIVE INSPIRATION FOR UNIQUE FABRIC PROJECTS. USE THIS GALLERY AS A JUMPING-OFF POINT FOR YOUR IMAGINATION.

CREATIVE SPIRIT DOLL

RIGHT ✦ When I saw this wonderful African face, I was inspired to create a doll that expresses my creative spirit—bold, sassy, unpredictable, colorful and flowing.

22" (56CM) LONG, COLLECTION OF THE ARTIST

JUNGLE FIRE

FAR RIGHT ✦ This elongated wall hanging incorporates silk, suede, fringe, hand-painted canvas squares, batik and a tree branch.

12" X 60" (30CM X 152CM), COLLECTION OF MYRA AND LUTHER ALEXANDER

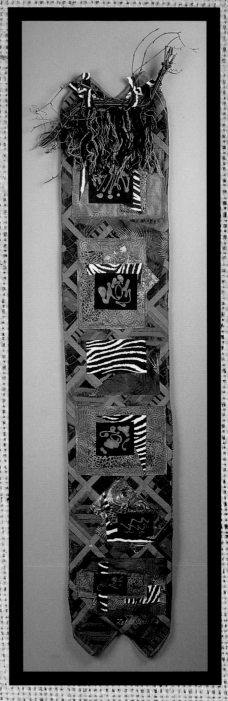

At craft fairs, tote bags are my most popular offering. I always marvel at the endless combinations of fabrics that can be achieved if you dare to try.

SAFARI TOTE WITH MUDCLOTH
TOP ✦ 22" X 24" (56CM X 61CM),
COLLECTION OF VALERIE MACK

PAINTED POCKET TOTES
BOTTOM ✦ 22" X 24" (56CM X 61CM),
COLLECTION OF THE ARTIST

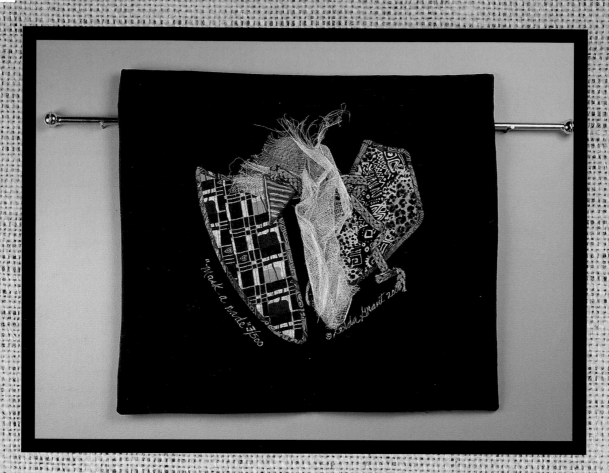

Mask-A-Rade

TOP ✦ This mask appears to dance on the canvas, therefore it gets its title from a twist on *masquerade*. This art piece has dual functions: it can be displayed as a wall hanging or you can remove the brass rod, insert a pillow form and use it as a pillow sham.

25" X 28" (64CM X 71CM), COLLECTION OF DR. AND MRS. LONNIE JENKINS

Waterfall

BOTTOM ✦ This wall sculpture was inspired by my desire to salvage this colorful scrap of fabric found in the bottom of a remnant box at a fabric store. The hand-dyed yarns and belt buckle added color, texture and movement to the piece.

22" X 36" (56CM X 91CM), COLLECTION OF MYRA AND LUTHER ALEXANDER

In My Dream

TOP ✦ I was inspired to create this wall hanging because I couldn't let go of my favorite pair of pants. So I recycled the fabric into an art piece.

26" X 58" (64CM X 147CM), COLLECTION OF DELORESE AMBROSE

Animal Fantasy

BOTTOM ✦ This piece was inspired by the idea of a story quilt. I imagined an amusement park at night after everyone has left. The animals step off the merry-go-round and scamper through the woods to have their own fun. They return just before dawn.

14" X 15" (36CM X 38CM), COLLECTION OF LAUWANA GAYE

ART PILLOWS

SAFARI COLLECTION

TOP ✦ These art pillows show how much fun you can have with animal prints and earth tones.

COLLECTION OF THE ARTIST

MOTIF COLLECTION

BOTTOM ✦ This group of art pillows displays the beauty of symbols in art. I especially like the dancers in the "window pane" pillow.

COLLECTION OF THE ARTIST

ART PILLOWS

KALEIDOSCOPE COLLECTION
TOP ✦ Luxurious textures and vibrant colors inspired this collection of art pillows.
COLLECTION OF THE ARTIST

FLOWERS AND FRUIT COLLECTION
BOTTOM ✦ These pillows were inspired by my favorite fruit, watermelon. The large pillow shows a melon plant growing wild. The small pillow features juicy, chilled slices ready to serve.
COLLECTION OF THE ARTIST

FABRIC FRAMES

These colorful mat board frames show how you can transform anything with fabric.

TROPICAL STYLE

TOP ✦ 8" X 11" (20CM X 28CM), COLLECTION OF BETTY RICHARDSON BROWN

AFRICAN TREASURE

BOTTOM ✦ 8" X 11" (20CM X 28CM), COLLECTION OF BETTY RICHARDSON BROWN

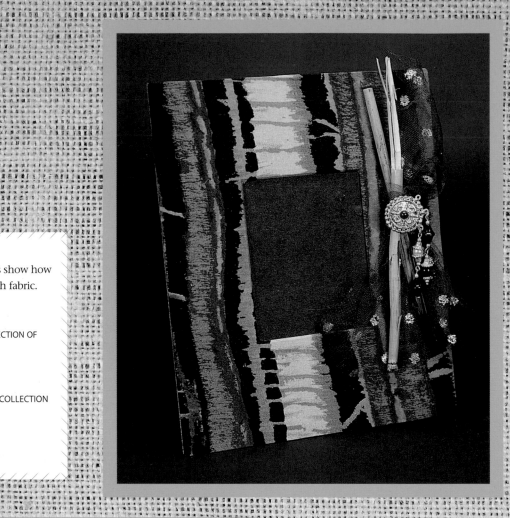

Mask

TOP ✦ This mixed-media collage shows how you can use fabric and embellishments the same way you use paint on a canvas.

13" X 22" (33CM X 56CM), COLLECTION OF THE ARTIST

Sister Queen

BOTTOM ✦ This fabric collage is one of several in my Sister series. I was inspired by the little ceramic heads

12" X 15" (30CM X 38CM), COLLECTION OF LAUWANA GAYE

Market Day

ABOVE ✦ Created to brighten a special room, this wall hanging demonstrates the dramatic power of color.

72" X 54" (183CM X 137CM), COLLECTION OF YVETTE WARNICK

Art Valance

RIGHT ✦ This custom window valance was made with raw silk and hand-dyed fiber embellishments. It was inspired by a smaller fringed wall hanging created five years earlier. Photo by Ernest Washington

14" X 166" (36CM X 422CM), COLLECTION OF BETTY RICHARDSON BROWN

templates

Elephant templates for the Elephant Safari Lamp Shade on page 70. These drawings have been reduced to 75%. Enlarge them to fit the dimensions of your lamp shade.

resources

✦ **Bag Lady & Company**
P.O. Box 5839
Atlanta, GA 30092
www.bagladyandco.com
1-800-842-4197
–fabric art, tote bags and workshops by Zelda Grant

✦ **Plaid Enterprises, Inc.**
3225 Westech Dr.
Norcross, GA 30092
www.plaidonline.com
1-800-842-4197
–decoupage mediums, glue, sealers, paints

✦ **Duncan Crafts**
5673 E. Shields Ave.
Fresno, CA 93727
www.duncancrafts.com
1-800-237-2642
–all-purpose craft glues and fabric paints

✦ **Coats & Clark**
P.O. Box 27067
Greenville, SC 29616
www.coatsandclark.com
1-800-648-1479
–general purpose threads

✦ **Fiskars, Inc.**
305 84th Ave. South
Wausau, WI 54401
www.fiskars.com
715-842-2091
–fabric scissors, paper cutters and sharpeners

✦ **STAMPede**
3 Terrace Dr.
Bethel, CT 06801
203-744-6187
stampede@rubberstampsforless.com
www.rubberstampsforless.com
–rubber stamps

✦ **C.M. Offray & Son Inc.**
360 Route 24
Chester, NJ 07930
908-879-4700
–decorative ribbons

✦ **Dharma Trading Co.**
P.O. Box 150916
San Rafael, CA 94915
1-800-542-5227
catalog@dharmatrading.com
www.dharmatrading.com
–fabric dyes, paints and fabric art products

✦

We must
learn to take what we have
to make what we want

We all
have some talent or gift
that can enhance our life
and the life of another

Whatever we
dedicate positive energy
and spirit to
will bring prosperity to life

To fully
realize what we are
we must be free to
fully express who we are

✦

ZELDA GRANT

Recommended Reading

Cameron, Julia. *The Artist's Way.* Los Angeles: Jeremy P. Tarcher/Perigree Books, 1992.

Diaz, Adriana. *Freeing the Creative Spirit.* San Francisco: HarperCollins Publishers, 1992.

Gawain, Shakti. *Creative Visualization.* Novato, CA: New World Library, 1995.

Maisel, Eric. *Fearless Creating.* New York: Jeremy P. Tarcher/Putnam, 1995.

May, Rollo. *The Courage to Create.* New York: W.W. Norton, 1974.

Shepard, Lisa. *African Accents.* Iola, WI: Krause Publications, 1999.

Warner, Sally. *Making Room for Making Art.* Chicago: Chicago Review Press, 1994.

index

a

Accent fabric, 67
African Mud Cloth Box, 52–55
African Treasure frame, 122
Animal Fantasy wall hanging, 119
Art pillows, 120–121. See also Pillow

b

Backing fabric, 43–44
Bag, drawstring, 86–91
Balance, 13
Basket, holiday, 47–51
Batik fabric, 24
Beads, wired, 75
Bias, cutting on the, 78
Birdhouse, 76–83
Bogolanfini, 54
Bookmark
    fabric, 34–37
    ribbon, 32
Box, storage, 52–55
Burlap, 88
Buttons, 13, 68,

c

Canvas, 102
Cards, greeting, 18–27
Caribbean Sky Pillow, 93–99
Casing, 90, 94
Chalk, tailor's, 72
Chenille rope, 74
Collage, 123
Contrast, 13
Cowrie Shell Holiday Basket, 47–51
Craft store, 14
Creative exercise, 15
Creative Spirit Doll, 116
Creative tools, 12
Creativity with fabrics, 12–13

d-e

Decoupage medium, 11, 37
Design principles, 12–13
Doll, Creative Spirit, 116
Dominance, 13
Drawstring bag, 86–91
Earrings, 14

Elephant Safari Lamp Shade, 70–75
Elephant template, 125
Embellishments, 14

f

Fabric
    accent, 67
    batik, 24
    burlap, 88
    canvas, 102
    finding, 13
    metallic, 48
    velveteen, 113
Fabric bookmark, 34–37
Fabric collage, 123
Far East Fabric Journal, 28–33
Feathers, 68
Flower accent, 61
Flowers and Fruit art pillows, 121
Folk Art Greeting Card, 18–27
Frame
    leopard print, 62–69
    mat board, 122
    shadow box, 40–45
    wooden, 64
Fusible web, 11, 72–73

g

Garland, 48
Glue, 11
Glue gun, 11
Gold lamé, 49
"Good eye," 12
Gradation, 13
Greeting cards, folk art, 18–27

h-i

Hand-sewing needles, 12, 115
Harmony, 13
Hem, 58, 89, 96, 107
Holiday basket, 47–51
Holiday Velvet Swag, 112–115
Hot glue guns, 11
Idea gallery, 25–27, 116–124
Imagination, 15
In My Dream wall hanging, 119
Interfacing, 11, 30, 102

j-l

Journal, fabric, 28–33
Jungle Fire wall hanging, 116
Kaleidoscope Collection art pillows, 121
Lamp shade, 70–75
Leopard Print Frame, 62–69
Liner, paper, 33
Lining
    for box, 55
    for velveteen, 114

m

Mask
    Mask-a-Rade, 118
    mixed media collage, 123
Mat board frames, 122
Materials, 11–12
Metallic fabric, 48
Metallic ribbon, 51
Mixed media collage, 123
Moon & Stars Drawstring Bag, 86–91
Mosaic-Tiled Birdhouse, 76–83
Motif Collection art pillow, 120
Mud cloth, 54, 117

n-o

Napkin rings, 106, 108
Needle, hand-sewing, 12, 115
Netting, 50
Organizing tips, 10–11
Ornaments, 50

p

Paint, fabric, 11
Paper liner, 33
Pillow, 93–99. See also Art pillows
Placemat, 106, 108
Pocket fold, 103
Pocket tote, 117
Potpourri, 59

r

Raffia trim, 83
Repetition, 13
Resources, 126
Rhythm, 13

Ribbon
    bookmark, 32
    metallic, 51
    sachet, 60
Rose & Eucalyptus Sachet, 56–61
Rubber stamp, 11, 106–107

s

Sachet, 56–61
Safari Collection art pillow, 120
Safari Tote With Mudcloth, 117
Sailboat Stationery Holder, 100–103
Scissors, 12
Seam ripper, 12
Seams, side, 90
Seascape Fabric Bookmark, 34–37
Selvage, 22
Sewing machine, 12
Shadow box, 38–45
Sister Queen fabric collage, 123
Stationery holder, 100–103
Storage box, 52–55
Swag, velvet, 112–115

t

Table linen set, 105–111
Table runner, 111
Tailor's chalk, 72
Tape, 39
Tassels, 114
Thrift stores, 13–14
Tools, 11–12
Totes, 117
Tropical Fish Table Linen Set, 105–111
Tropical style frame, 122

v-z

Valance, window, 124
Wall hangings, 116, 119
Waterfall wall sculpture, 118
Window valance, 124
Wired beads, 75
Workspace, 10–11
X-acto knife, 39, 66
Zebra Stripe Shadow Box, 38–45

A man's gift maketh room for him, and bringeth him before great men.

Biblical Proverb

Get Creative with
Northlight Books!

These books and other fine North Light titles are available from your local art & craft retailer, bookstore, online supplier or by calling 1-800-221-5831.

Learn how to create exquisitely detailed animal sculptures that are full of personality. Inside you'll find 10 charming projects, including bluebirds, white-tailed fawns, basset hounds, rabbits, bears and more. You'll even learn how to model animals to look like bronze or jade. 0-89134-955-3, paperback, 128 pages, #31428-K

You can create your own tabletop fountains and add beautiful accents to your living room, bedroom, kitchen and garden. These 15 gorgeous step-by-step projects make it easy, using everything from lava rock and bamboo to shells and clay pots. 1-58180-103-3, paperback, 128 pages, #31791-K

Make unique, expressive gifts with rubber stamps in combination with polymer clay, shrink plastic, handmade paper and more. Each project demonstrates a specific technique, then goes on to include stunning examples of how each can be combined or refined to produce a sophisticated piece of art. 1-58180-081-9, paperback, 128 pages, #31667-K

Judy Barker introduces you to the basics of stenciling and embossing attractive greeting cards. You'll also learn how to embellish them with foil, polymer clay, shrink plastic and more. It's everything you need to make one-of-a-kind cards for family and friends alike. 0-89134-997-9, paperback, 128 pages, #31613-K